GLIMPSES OF KYOTO LIFE

Glimpses of Kyoto Life

by John Lowe

Pitt Rivers Museum, University of Oxford

1996

Published with the assistance of the Idlewild Trust

Published in conjunction with the exhibition
Glimpses of Kyoto Life: The John Lowe Collection
held at the Pitt Rivers Museum, University of Oxford
from 1 November 1996 to 1 November 1997.

Copyright © John Lowe 1996.

ISBN: 0 902793 37 3

Printed by Stephen Austin and Sons Ltd, Hertford.

Front cover: Detail of a scroll-painting by Hoen (1804–67) depicting the autumn maples at Tsutenkyo Bridge, Tofuku-ji temple, Kyoto. (1996.17.192)

Back cover: Detail of an embroidered and painted silk *kosode*, an earlier type of kimono. Made in Kyoto in the Edo period. (1996.17.103)

For my children

Miki, Judith,
Dominic and Mark

who have shared Kyoto with me

More and more
Do I yearn for
The capital I have left.
O how I envy
Waves that can return.

Ariwara no Narihira (AD 825–880)

Foreword

It gives me great pleasure to write a Foreword to this book. When John Lowe first approached me with an offer to give the Pitt Rivers Museum some Japanese material, he described it as 'the contents of three houses'. For him, indeed, it has been 'not so much a collection, more a way of life', for many of the objects he has given us were for his practical, daily use. The donor of the Museum's founding collection, General Pitt Rivers, was ahead of his time in recognizing the importance of collecting just such 'ordinary and everyday' objects before they disappeared forever. This idea has continued to underpin the Museum's collecting policy and has enriched its collections, for it is now acknowledged that the ordinary object of today becomes a priceless record for the cultural anthropologist of tomorrow.

There are, however, items of outstanding beauty in what inevitably has become 'the Lowe collection': among them, a number of scroll paintings (a detail from one of which graces the front cover of this book) and an embroidered and painted Edo-period silk *kosode* (a detail of which graces the back cover). Such items will enhance the Museum's other notable Japanese holdings: the Noh masks and samurai armour from the Original Pitt Rivers Collection, for example, and the Herman Gunther collection of netsuke, which are on permanent display in the Museum. As those familiar with his published work will know, John Lowe has a profound interest in and knowledge of Japanese crafts and craftsmen. Although he does not like to think of himself as a collector, he accumulates objects with the eye of a connoisseur.

John Lowe's generosity has included not only the gift of his collection, but also the manuscript of this book. Included among the illustrations in the body of the book are several from his son Mark's collection of slides and photographs of Japanese crafts and craftsmen at work, which has also been given to the Museum. Having lived in Japan for a number of years, John Lowe writes about the country from the personal viewpoint of one who has experienced the meeting of cultures at first hand.

I take this opportunity to thank John and Mark Lowe for their gifts, which will benefit both scholars and visitors to the Museum for years to come. We are most grateful to them.

Schuyler Jones

Acknowledgements

I am grateful to Schuyler Jones for inviting me to write this memoir of my years in Kyoto, and to the staff of the Pitt Rivers Museum for the help they have given me. As always, my friend and editor Richard Ward has added so much more than he has taken away. My thanks also to Sally Owen, and to Hideko Fujii, Takashi Mine, and Tetsuo and Hideko Nakatsukasa who always give me so much help in Japan.

John Lowe

Contents

Foreword	vii
Acknowledgements	viii
List of Illustrations	x
Periods of Japanese History	xi
1. Introduction	1
2. Everyday Life in Kyoto	5
3. Religion	10
4. Tea Drinking	14
5. Tea Ceremony	16
6. Incense	18
7. Food and Drink	20
8. Paper	23
9. Calligraphy and Seals	24
10. Mingei	27
11. Mizuhiki	29
12. A Last Glimpse	31
Suggested Further Reading	33
About the Author	35

List of Illustrations

Plates I to XVI between pp. 4 and 5.

Plate I. Sushi bar, Kyoto.
Plate II. Boxes of *o-sushi*.
Plate III. Broom shop, Kyoto.
Plate IV. Chopsticks.
Plate V. Papering an umbrella.
Plate VI. Drying umbrellas.
Plates VII–VIII. Paper lantern making.
Plate IX. Thermos.
Plate X. Soy-sauce pot.
Plates XI–XIII. Tea-bowls.
Plates XIV–XV. Teacups.
Plate XVI. Incense boxes.

Plates XVII to XXXII between pp. 20 and 21.

Plates XVII–XVIII. Scroll-paintings.
Plate XIX. Seal and seal-case.
Plate XX. Lacquerware.
Plate XXI. Dish.
Plate XXII. Shells.
Plate XXIII. Bowls and box.
Plate XXIV. Travelling tea ceremony set.
Plate XXV. Sake bottle.
Plate XXVI. Dish.
Plate XXVII–XXVIII. Bottles.
Plate XXIX–XXXI. *Mizuhiki* envelopes.
Plate XXXII. Ship of Fortune.

All photographs by Malcolm Osman of the Pitt Rivers Museum, except Plates I to IV and VIII by Mark Lowe and Plates V to VII by the author. All illustrations copyright © Pitt Rivers Museum, University of Oxford.

Periods of Japanese History, from AD 552 to the Present

Asuka 552–645
Nara 645–794
Heian 794–1185
Kamakura 1185–1392
Muromachi 1392–1568
Momoyama 1568–1600
Edo 1600–1868
Meiji 1868–1912
Taisho 1912–1926
Showa 1926–1989
Heisei 1989–

1

Introduction

Anthropology is generally perceived as the study of small societies, once misleadingly called 'primitive', living in remote areas of the world. The discipline includes the collection and study of the implements and household utensils used by people in such societies in the practice of their religion and culture and in their daily lives. The Pitt Rivers Museum, whose collections number more than a million objects, is one of the world's greatest repositories of such artefacts, brought back from every corner of the globe by explorers, travellers and professional anthropologists. At first glance, the galleries, crowded with tools, weapons, and a great variety of simple craft objects, seem to reinforce the view that anthropology is concerned only with the study of small tribal groups.

How then do five hundred Japanese objects, mostly dating from the second half of the twentieth century, fit into the collections of the Pitt Rivers Museum? The basic answer is that anthropology is concerned with the study of mankind throughout history, so that objects that reveal the culture of Japan are just as relevant as those which help towards the understanding of the world-view of a small tribe in Borneo or Guatemala. Furthermore, in the case of the Japanese, it might be argued that they are, in fact, the largest tribal society in the world. They are an exceptionally homogeneous people, bound together by living traditions, a deeply cultural language and mythical beliefs about their pure origins and their difference from all other peoples.

Japan cut herself off almost entirely from the rest of the world from 1639 to 1854. That long period of isolation still has a deep effect on the Japanese, despite all the modernization of the postwar years. A few years ago a national poll revealed that 70% of the Japanese people had no wish to have any dealings with foreigners; the word for foreigner, significantly, being *gaijin*, meaning 'outside person'. Another study, of the large Japanese community in New York, showed that about 90% of that population socialized only with other Japanese. And those bulging suitcases one sees Japanese tourists manoeuvring around the world often do not contain clothes, but large quantities of Japanese food.

Most of the objects in the collection I donated to the Pitt Rivers Museum earlier this year come from Kyoto, the ancient capital of Japan. This city has fascinated me for thirty years, during thirteen of which I lived there. In this brief introduction I should like to put the collection into perspective by outlining something of the history of the city and of my own life there between 1978 and 1991.

Emperor Kammu's (737–806) new capital, Heiankyo, 'Capital of Peace and Tranquillity', was founded just over twelve hundred years ago in 794. Informally, it was called Kyoto, 'Capital City', and by the eleventh century this had become its official name. From the sixth century onwards, Japan had been deeply under the influence of China, and Heiankyo's layout followed that of the T'ang capital, Chang'an, today's Xi'an. Smaller than the Chinese capital, but larger than the three preceding Japanese capitals (themselves all built after Chang'an's plan), Heiankyo was laid out in a chequerboard pattern, *jyobo-sei*. Its original wide roads running north and south still exist, crossed by a network of smaller streets and lanes, and much of the character of the city comes from the contrast between the formal spaciousness of its great avenues and the intimacy of its back streets.

Kyoto was continually ravaged by war and natural disasters, fire being the greatest destroyer of a city built entirely of wood. By the early sixteenth century, war had reduced the centre of Kyoto to ruins, of which St Francis Xavier gave an eyewitness account in a letter he wrote in 1549. The city was rebuilt, with considerable alterations to Emperor Kammu's plans, by Toyotome Hideyoshi (1537–98), a great war-lord who finally unified Japan in the late sixteenth century. So little now remains of Emperor Kammu's city. Though there are a few temples and shrines that still have their ancient names, they do not have their original buildings. There is, however, one surviving fragment of Kammu's imperial palace grounds. This is a small lake to the south of Nijo castle, once part of Kammu's pleasure park, the 'Divine Spring Garden'. The palace, burnt down many times, was finally destroyed in 1788, and the present imperial palace was built on a different site in 1790, in the centre of the enlarged town. The present buildings only date from 1855. Many other important buildings in Kyoto have been rebuilt or heavily restored several times, though for the most part the new buildings reproduce the earlier designs. The Golden Pavilion was burnt down by a deranged Buddhist monk in 1950, and the exquisite building we admire today is a perfect replica completed in 1955. The city remains steeped in tradition, yet has experienced continual growth and change; today provoking fierce controversy between conservationists and developers.

Although Tokyo became the new capital of Japan and the emperor moved there at the beginning of the Meiji period in 1868, for the Japanese people Kyoto remains the cultural and religious heart of the country. It is the headquarters of the leading Buddhist sects and is the location of many of Japan's most ancient and famous Shinto shrines. It is also the home of many traditional arts and crafts, from tea ceremony to Noh drama, and its craftspeople make the finest kimonos and folding fans as well as the finest sets of boxwood combs produced for each new empress and for the most important Shinto shrines.

Kyoto likes to boast that it has one thousand temples and one thousand shrines, and these symbolic numbers are not far from the truth. I have been visiting Kyoto at least once a year for thirty years, and despite having walked and bicycled its streets in search of every place of interest, I now accept that I shall never find everything worth seeing. One lifetime is not enough for this inexhaustible city, whose three-star sights must be numbered in dozens, not counting the fascinating traditional festivals that seem to take place on almost every day of the year.

I first visited Kyoto in 1967, travelling there from Tokyo where I was mounting an exhibition of Queen Victoria's coronation robes at a large department store. Kyoto was a simpler, quieter place in those days, with only a few Western-style hotels, and with little traffic in the streets except for taxis. I remember particularly that the main street, Kawaramachi-dori, was lined with shops specializing in Japanese traditional crafts, selling everything from exquisite dolls to handsome boards for go, the Japanese board game. Today, most of these shops have been replaced by boutiques and fast-food joints, and some more leisurely restaurants. While waiting for Japanese friends in the lobby of the new Kyoto Hotel in 1995 I noticed another change. In the past, the lobby would have been crowded with foreign tourists. Now, I was the only non-Japanese in sight. The strength of the yen has drastically reduced tourism to Japan.

Each time I visited Kyoto I became more fascinated both by its past and by its contemporary life. I longed to live there and patience was finally rewarded in 1978 when I was offered a visiting professorship at Doshisha, the oldest and largest private university in the city. At the same time I was commissioned to write a book about traditional Kyoto crafts. All my career I had been involved with crafts. I had worked in the woodwork and ceramics departments of the Victoria & Albert Museum, and after working in two other museums, had become the founding principal of West Dean College, which is devoted to teaching a wide variety of crafts. Already by 1978 I had become interested in Japanese crafts. I had collected a few objects on each of my visits and I had developed the idea of writing a book that would present detailed studies of a number of the traditional crafts of Kyoto, looking at their history and their place in Japanese life and including an exact written and photographic account of all the processes involved.

Such a book required a great deal of photography. My son, Mark, was a skilled amateur photographer and he agreed to come out to Japan to work with me on the book. He spent six months working on the project, and when I saw the results I realised that there was nothing amateur about his photography. He has now given the Pitt Rivers Museum the collection of colour transparencies and black-and-white photographs he took for the book, including many of crafts not included in that publication. The collection of Mark's photographs makes a perfect companion to the collection of objects.

Mark and I set our sights high, aiming to study the work of the best craftsmen in Kyoto, from those who worked for the master of the fan-makers guild to the family who made boxwood combs for the imperial family. Our problem was to get introductions to these people. There were two particular difficulties. First, there were too many foreigners in Japan who claimed to be working on books. Many of them never produced anything, merely wasting the time of very busy people and creating a feeling of distrust among many of the craftsmen. Secondly, many leading Japanese craftsmen were besieged for interviews by Japanese journalists writing articles for newspapers and magazines. Often, these interviews also wasted the craftsmen's time and prevented them from getting on with their work and earning their modest living.

About the time we started doing the research for the book, several Kyoto craftsmen were considering making a charge for giving interviews. 'You see,' said one craftsman to my son, 'while you are taking photographs, we shall waste a whole morning.' Of course, the last thing we wanted was for them to stop work. We wanted to spend the maximum amount of time possible observing them *at* work. To begin with many of the craftsmen found this hard to believe, but eventually we broke through the barriers of formality and misunderstanding and they found that it was possible to continue working while explaining what they were doing and answering our questions.

I have never ceased to wonder how such perfect works of craftsmanship can be created in the crowded, ill-lit and often extremely scruffy workshops of Kyoto. It is the same elsewhere, as I know from having visited a paper-umbrella maker in Gifu, a town not far from Kyoto, whose craftspeople specialize in making lanterns and umbrellas. This man's workshop was very small and, apart from a small area by the door, the whole floor was covered to a depth of four inches or so in all the bits and pieces he had discarded over the years. Indeed, it turned out to be worse than that for he had not even swept up when he took over the workshop from his father. It all looked like rubbish to me, but when I asked if I might stand behind him in the middle of this sea of off-cuts he reverently cleared a small space in which he placed two telephone directories. I could stand on those he said. Stand? I balanced there precariously for fifty minutes, but I did get a perfect view of the whole intricate process of papering an umbrella (see Plate V).

Of course, no Japanese craftsman really believes that any foreigner can understand what he is doing. Sometimes, the craft processes were complex; others, explained in hushed tones, were basic processes our school carpenter had explained to me when I was ten years old. One finds this with craftsmen all over the world. If a man spends his whole working life repeating the same process over and over again, sooner or later he finds it necessary to surround it with a certain mystique. It is a pose by no means limited to craftsmen.

It is the degree of specialization that gives perfection to traditional Japanese crafts; that, and the total dedication of every craftsman. Making a folding fan involves some thirty separate processes, from cutting the bamboo to fitting the two outside sticks. This work is carried out by as many as six specialist craftsmen, some working in their own homes and sending on bundles of half-finished fans to the next workshop. For us this meant that we had to visit each workshop in turn, besides spending a lot of time at the master's shop, where he showed us the many different kinds of fan: for tea ceremony, for dancing, for kabuki, for Noh and for the sumo referee.

After two years at Doshisha, I stayed on in Kyoto to finish *Japanese Crafts*, and to become a full-time writer working on a book called *Into Japan*. I also began to write articles on many different aspects of Japanese life—from esoteric Buddhism to the *geisha-san* of Pontocho—for many of Japan's English-language magazines and newspapers. This work gave me marvellous opportunities for investigating anything and everything that interested me. And so I continued living in Kyoto, in places as diverse as a Zen Buddhist temple and an enchanting tea ceremony pavilion on the slopes of the eastern mountains.

I must end this introduction with a brief account of how I made the collection of Japanese objects I have given to the Pitt Rivers Museum. Some objects were deliberately collected—the sculptures and paintings, for example, and the many tea bowls and incense boxes, in which it must seem as if I have an obsessive interest. With these exceptions, however, it is not so much a collection as a way of life. I am not an anthropologist, but as a result of the experience of working with the staff of the Pitt Rivers to help accession the collection into the Museum, I have come to feel that perhaps throughout my career I have been one unconsciously. And if, as it has been said, 'the proper study of mankind is man', a variety of disciplines may involve a strand of anthropology. When I worked at the Victoria & Albert Museum I enjoyed the aesthetic qualities of Chippendale furniture and Chelsea porcelain, but the first articles I wrote about them concerned the history of eating and drinking, for I found the things interesting more as documents of human behaviour than as beautiful objects.

Almost from the moment I arrived in Japan I began to try to solve what one might call the Japanese enigma. Every traditional Japanese object seemed to offer clues to understanding some aspect of Japanese life. While I did do some deliberate collecting, the futon, the *nemaki* (traditional sleeping garment), the many pieces of tableware, the sake cups and chopsticks, these I bought for daily use. Indeed, common sense and lack of space dictated a Japanese lifestyle. With only two small rooms, apart from the kitchen area, a Western bed and cluttering furniture would have left me no room to work, or to put up my family and friends. I found the Japanese way of life convenient and comfortable, with the great advantage that all the time it was teaching me lessons about the Japanese.

I well remember buying my first piece of Japanese craftsmanship during my first visit to Japan. In a small shop off Tokyo's Ginza, which specialized in equipment for tea ceremony, there was a shelf of black bowls. They looked identical to me, except that the one I had decided to purchase, a modern raku tea bowl, touched with splashes of cream and red, cost only 5000 yen (Y), then about £5, while the bowl at the far end cost Y250,000 (£250). I told the owner of the shop that I could not detect the slightest difference between the two bowls. He smiled and, turning over the expensive bowl, pointed at the illustrious seal-signature on the base. 'That is the difference,' he said. It was my first lesson in the vagaries of the Japanese craft world. And while my bowl had a signature, though a much less illustrious one, it came only in a cardboard box, while the other bowl came in a beautiful wooden box with elegant *himo* ties of braided cord.

It was my first lesson, and one that I never forgot.

Plate I. A Kyoto sushi bar and its owner, Yoshihisa Futaya-san. (JL532)

Plate II. Boxes, *o-bento*, of takeaway, cheap *o-sushi*, available in many shops in Kyoto. (JL495)

Plate III. The famous broom shop by Sanjo bridge, Kyoto. (JL66)

Plate IV. A variety of chopsticks for sale in a Kyoto shop. (JL122)

Plate V. Toshikazu Masuda-san papering a traditional umbrella in his Gifu workshop. (JL611)

Plate VI. Oiled paper umbrellas drying in the sun, Gifu. (JL609)

Plate VII. Laying the paper on the frame of a lantern, Gifu. (JL488)

Plate VIII. Painting Chinese characters on a paper lantern, in a lantern and umbrella shop in Kyoto. (JL487)

Plate IX. A Japanese thermos, for refilling the small teapots used for serving green tea. (1996.17.212)

Plate X. A soy-sauce pot, in porcelain, with lid and saucer. *Shoyu* is the basic Japanese flavouring. (1996.17.234)

Plate XI. Porcelain tea-bowl for tea ceremony, painted with a formal pattern. (1996.17.24)

Plate XII. Tea-bowl of rough red raku ware, particularly popular for tea ceremony. (1996.17.37)

Plate XIII. Pottery tea-bowl for tea ceremony, painted with a pattern of autumn leaves. (1996.17.32)

Plate XIV. A pair of tall pottery cups for tea. (1996.17.216)

Plate XV. A pair of pottery teacups: the larger on the left for the man, the smaller for the woman. (1996.17.208)

2

Everyday Life in Kyoto

I lived for some time in a small apartment in Shimogamo. This is a pleasant, old-fashioned residential area of the city, running down the east side of the Kamogawa River, with quiet streets lined with large wooden houses and spacious gardens. A taxi driver told me it had been a favourite location for samurai movies until after the Second World War when many of the houses were enclosed by ugly walls of grey concrete and the historical illusion was destroyed.

My landlady had inherited a large house on a corner site. She had demolished the old family home and built a modern house with a small apartment block behind it. Eight of the apartments were contained in a two-storey building, but one half of this rose another storey to accommodate two additional apartments. Her neighbours were much displeased, their protests probably expressed through a chilling silence. This was the first apartment block to be built in the immediate neighbourhood and the third storey was above the local building line. Bowing to neighbourhood opinion, my landlady left the two upper apartments unlet for two years, an empty gesture of apology and one that I suspect was included in the original costing. So that is how I came to occupy a brand new apartment two years after it was built.

When I first rented an apartment there, my position as visiting professor at Doshisha University was sufficient guarantee that I would pay the rent and be a responsible tenant, without further references. When I returned three years later, however, and wanted to rent an apartment again, I was no longer at Doshisha and everything was different. Despite the fact that I had been a sober and reliable tenant, and in any other country in the world would have been welcomed as an old friend, I might as well have been a vagrant. In Japanese society one's identity is professional, not personal. No longer a visiting professor, I was merely a foreigner, who might vanish in the night without paying the rent. There was an apartment vacant, but my former landlady now required a solid Japanese reference.

I racked my brains and suddenly remembered that one of my graduate students had recently obtained a lectureship at some obscure private university near Kyoto. Fortunately, my landlady knew the university and said that she would accept his guarantee if I could get him to put his seal on the contract. I telephoned my friend. He was happy to guarantee the lease, but he could not come that day. He suggested that I went to the nearest shop selling unregistered seals, bought one with his family name and, with his spoken permission, seal the document in his absence. To my surprise, my landlady was content with this procedure. I went off and bought a seal, committed my friend as guarantor and, after paying a huge amount of key-money, was once again the tenant of an apartment in Kamo Haitsu. The penalties for the misuse of seals in Japan are Draconian, but their actual use appears extraordinarily casual. The contrast is very Japanese.

One morning, a few weeks later, I was getting ready to go shopping. My door-bell rang. It was my landlady with a beautifully wrapped parcel. She explained that the people who lived opposite were starting to rebuild their house and, acting as their go-between, she was bringing a present (one of which was sent to all the neighbours) to mark their regret for the nuisance that the work would cause. The parcel contained a *castella*, a popular kind of light sponge cake said to have been introduced by the Portuguese in the sixteenth century. I asked my landlady if our neighbours were going to build a more modern and convenient house.

Plate XVI. Pottery incense boxes; a view showing the decoration on the lids. The circular box decorated with cranes (top left) is Korean celadon ware. (1996.17.48)

This, she explained, was out of the question. The family were well-known kimono designers and therefore they must live in a traditional house. And so it was. For three months I watched the building of what seemed to be an exact replica of their previous home, and when the house was finished their former garden was replaced, stone by stone and tree by tree.

The neighbourhood was like a village, complete with its own high street. In the middle of the high street was a covered market with stalls selling every kind of food: meat, fish and vegetables, and a variety of Japanese specialities, such as fresh and fried tofu (bean curd), cold *tempura* (deep-fried fish and vegetables), Japanese pickles, cakes of bean paste and bean jam, and a selection of green teas. Nearly every neighbourhood in Kyoto has its covered market, large or small, but similar foods are also sold at small speciality shops. Even in the market, each stall sells only one kind of produce, just as restaurants in Japan tend to serve one variety of food. Japan is a land of specialization in everything.

I went first to the chicken counter, where neatly dissected pieces of chicken were displayed on trays in a refrigerated cabinet. A child could grow up in Kyoto without having any idea what a chicken looks like. All meat shops in Japan present the meat in this fragmented form, which goes some way to disguise its origins from squeamish customers. The chickens are delivered whole and cut up in the back of the shop behind closed doors. You can, in fact, buy a whole chicken, if you ask. I did just that once in the company of a Japanese friend. When the chicken-seller presented the bird for my approval, my friend turned away. She later told me that she had never before seen a whole dead chicken, and only very few live ones. This way of selling meat is no doubt due in part at least to the fact that that is how it is cooked in Japan, but it may also have roots in the long tradition of Buddhist vegetarianism, which for centuries has frowned on the eating of meat. Wild boar has long been a popular dish in Japan, long before other meats became common, but to salve Buddhist consciences it was often referred to as 'mountain whale'.

I always liked the vegetable stall, partly for its beautiful display of Japanese and Western vegetables and fruit, but more for the bustling couple who owned it. They were real Kyotoites, who talked non-stop in a mixture of standard Japanese and Kyoto-ben, the local dialect. Such local dialects are found all over Japan, and Kyoto-ben, with its intricate constructions and its own vocabulary, reflects the particular character of the city and its polite and elegant way of life. Of course, as the only foreigner in the neighbourhood, I was well-known in the market, and the woman at the vegetable stall had made herself my self-appointed adviser. A man doing his own shopping, and a *gaijin*, or foreigner, at that, clearly needed all the help he could get. I always came with my own shopping list, and I always went away with what the *oba-chan* chose for me. We always parted with the same joke. I thanked her with my only words of Kyoto-ben, '*Okini-domo*' (thank you very much). 'Ah!', she would laugh raucously, 'the real Kyoto man'.

Then I had a stroke of good luck. My expensive English shoes badly needed mending. The trouble was that in general in modern Japan shoes have become a cheap throwaway commodity. There were men squatting on the pavement in the centre of Kyoto who carried out rough-and-ready repairs, but I did not feel like entrusting my shoes to them. I was in despair until that day when at the far end of the high street I noticed one of those shops so forlorn-looking that it is hard to tell if it is still in business. In the window was a saddle, and close by two pairs of wooden lasts on one of which there was what looked like a pair of fancy Edwardian shoes. Peering through the window, I saw no sign of activity inside. My shoes demanded attention, however, and I pushed open the door and entered the discouragingly dark, dusty and silent interior of the shop. I waited, shuffling my feet noisily to attract attention, and at last a door opened and an old man appeared. He looked as surprised as I felt, but now I was committed. I apologized for troubling him, showed him my shoes and asked if he could repair them. He asked me if the shoes were English and said that they were the best-made shoes he had seen in years. And yes, he could sole and heel them, but it would be expensive. I held my breath while he calculated the price. He then named a figure that was about as outdated as the shoes in the window. I accepted, and when I returned a week later he had repaired them to the highest standard. I tried to thank him, but he assured me that it had given him great pleasure to work on shoes of such rare quality.

I also wanted a new kitchen knife, so I made my way back up the street to the ironmonger-cum-general stores, which sold just about everything for building and equipping a house. The crowded stock on view—and there was apparently far more behind the scenes—provided an illuminating lesson about Japanese life: in addition to the enormous variety of tablewares there was a range of ingenious telescopic gadgets for hanging-out washing or hanging-up clothes in houses and apartments where space was at a premium. The shop was run by a helpful father and son, and I always needed their help as invariably I wanted some obscure household fitting for which I did not know the Japanese word.

The knife presented no problem as examples of several types were on display. There is an almost unending variety of Japanese knives including, for example, one small knife made to gut a particular type of fish caught only in the neighbourhood of a particular Japanese town. I wanted a vegetable knife with a medium-length triangular blade, which of all Japanese knives serves the most purposes. The son came over to help and passed me a knife. 'Too light,' I said, and I thought I saw a glimmer of respect in his eyes as he turned and headed to the back of the shop. He returned with a beautifully made knife at five times the price of the other one. 'Perfect,' I said, reflecting on what marvellous knives the Japanese make. 'You'll need one of these,' he said, passing me a small Western-style sharpening gadget. I looked again at the elegant knife. 'Made in Sweden' it said on its Japanese-style handle. Well, even Japanese craftsmen must now compete in the international marketplace and the Japanese housewife is only human. Japanese knives are works of high craftsmanship, but they are brutes to sharpen; fine for the sushi-cook, but not so convenient for the modern Japanese woman struggling to make lunch with two children playing around her feet.

My next stop was the local stationery shop, which sold everything from space-saving filing systems to Snoopy post cards. Snoopy was all the rage then, but with the opening of Tokyo Disneyland he has since been pushed out of favour by Mickey Mouse. The shop was run by a very old couple, a situation all too common with many small specialist shops in Japan. In many cases the shop is the only livelihood of such people and they carry on, often until they die. These shops, which have served their neighbourhoods so well, are fast disappearing and being replaced by American-style convenience stores, which while convenient do not offer the same personal service or range of goods.

That day, I had gone to the stationery shop because one of my former graduate students was getting married. I had been asked to her wedding and I had to send a present of money in the correct style of gift envelope (Plates XXIX–XXXI). There was a rack in the shop displaying a large variety of envelopes, ranging from richly decorated types for celebratory occasions to the sombre black-and-white ones in which one sends 'incense money' to the bereaved, to help pay for the cost of the funeral. A wedding envelope must have a lot of red and gold, or nowadays may be a more upmarket envelope in which the *mizuhiki* strings are tied into pretty posies. The Japanese craftsman must adapt to the demands of new customers, especially those of young girls who have little taste for the traditional.

My last call of the morning was to the neighbourhood beer-man, who delivered at all hours of the day and night in his light truck. He was a delightful, ever-cheerful small man, who always wore the kind of traditional canvas apron one can see in Hokusai prints. He and his wife ran a crowded liquor store in a narrow lane off the high street, and he raced around the neighbourhood humping heavy crates containing twenty large bottles of beer up garden paths and the steep stairs of apartment houses. Later, when I moved to another quite distant neighbourhood, he insisted on continuing to deliver to me.

Having ordered a fresh supply of beer and some Californian wine—the best value in Japan at that time—I returned home for some lunch. It was hot, so with a *bento*, or box, of takeaway *o-sushi* (see Plate II) I had a large glass of that favourite Japanese summer drink, cold *mugi-cha*, barley tea. The *o-sushi* was delicious: slices of raw fish perched on fingers of vinegared rice, *nigiri*, and rolls of tuna fish or cucumber in rice, neatly wrapped in sheets of cultivated seaweed, *makizushi*. This type of *o-sushi*, called *nigirizushi*, comes from the Kanto region around Tokyo, though it is popular all over Japan. The local sushi of Kyoto and the Kansai region is made in one large block, *hakozushi*, often in a special wooden box, or spread on a large plate, *chivashizushi*, as a communal dish. Many sushi bars now only serve sushi in the Tokyo style, and are extremely expensive, though a cheaper type of sushi bar can be found in Kyoto and elsewhere. Here the sushi cooks stand in the middle of a long, oval, revolving counter on which they place small saucers, with coloured rims indicating different prices, each with two pieces of sushi or four of the cheaper varieties. The customers sit on stools at the revolving counter with its saucers of sushi and choose whatever takes their fancy. As they get up to leave, an attendant counts the empty saucers and scribbles a bill, which is paid at the cash desk by the door. When I am downtown, I always treat myself to lunch at one of these *kurukuru-zushi*.

I wanted to buy a gas cooker with a large oven, and that afternoon a salesman from the Osaka Gas Company was coming to advise me. Japanese home cooking only requires two gas rings and a grill, which are standard equipment in every Japanese kitchen. Some Japanese housewives, however, have taken to baking Western-style cakes and bread, so a range of ovens has been introduced, all of them just large enough for one cake but totally inadequate for those whole chickens I had recently discovered. Like other foreigners I could have imported a large gas cooker from the United States, but I refused to believe that a practical roasting oven could not be obtained in Japan. Life in Kyoto was punctuated with these small cross-cultural battles.

At three o'clock sharp, a pleasant, middle-aged salesman arrived. After I had served him the obligatory cup of green tea, he produced a fat catalogue. He thumbed through it until he found the page he was looking for, placed the open catalogue on the table in front of me, and stabbing with an authoritative finger said, 'That is the gas cooker you want.' He was pointing at a coloured illustration the size of a small postage stamp. In fact, all that was clearly legible was the price. At a glance I could see that it was easily the most expensive of the sixteen gas cookers illustrated—postage-stamp size—on the open pages. I peered at the brief description below the picture. It told one nothing; nor really did the minuscule picture.

'This looks interesting,' I said, trying to be polite. 'Now, where in Kyoto can I see one?' 'I'm afraid you can't see it anywhere,' he replied. 'This is a special model, only available to order.'

'Well, could you give me the specifications? I'm mostly interested in the size of the oven. What are the internal dimensions?'

The salesman looked blank. 'I don't know,' he said.

I was growing less 'Japanese' every second. 'But look here,' I said. 'This is an extremely expensive gas cooker. Do you really expect me to buy it on the strength of that tiny illustration?'

'I assure you,' said the expert, 'that is exactly the gas cooker you need; perfect for your cooking.'

In every area of life, from medical treatment to the purchase of gas cookers, the Japanese accept the word of authority without question and without making a personal choice. The last thing they would ever do is question the qualifications of an authority. I was not structured that way and I asked the salesman, knowing the answer perfectly well, 'Tell me Fujikawa-san, how many evenings each week do you cook the supper?' Of course, he didn't cook supper, or breakfast either, but I was the loser. I bought the gas cooker simply because there was no choice, and to be fair to authority, although the oven was hardly spacious, the chicken fitted in quite well and roasted to perfection.

Later in the afternoon my two grown-up sons, who were living with me at the time, returned home. One had been teaching English conversation to a recalcitrant class all afternoon. The other had been taking photographs in the cramped workshop of a fan painter. Both were hungry. We decided to eat at the neighbourhood Chinese restaurant. It was a simple place, but the food was excellent and the family always welcoming. As with all those things that Japan has borrowed from abroad—from the Chinese script in the sixth century to the Western household appliances of the twentieth century—everything is adapted to fit the Japanese way of life and Japanese taste. The spring rolls, fried chicken and fried rice served in the little local restaurant were recognizably Chinese, yet also subtly different; less fatty, blander, and in general more easily digestible. Such Japanese–Chinese food also goes very well with Japanese beer, which has largely replaced sake as the national drink. Many hotels now open a roof-top beer garden during the hot and humid summer months.

It had been a tiring day for all three of us, and we decided to end it in the local *sento* or public bathhouse. These institutions can trace their origins back to early medieval times, when the authorities of the great temples built large steam baths for the poor of the neighbourhood. Even in this century many houses lacked a bathroom, so every evening the members of the household would go to the local bathhouse where, for a few yen, they could all soak in very hot water. With the general improvement in domestic plumbing, bathhouses have been closing, but they retain some popularity as social centres. Public bathing is deeply rooted in Japanese culture, though since Western prudery began to influence Japanese attitudes to nudity in the late nineteenth century, the sexes are now separated, and on the men's side it is noticeable that as they walk around they hold a towel in front of their genitals. A hundred years ago the Japanese had no inhibitions about nudity.

We went home to collect towels, soap and shampoo, and after paying the fee we entered the men's changing room. One chooses a locker, which contains an empty basket. In this one puts one's clothes and valuables before locking them away with a key on an elastic band, which one puts around one's wrist. Entering the actual bathhouse, one first ignores the various baths themselves and squats by the wall beneath a small shower to wash oneself, including one's hair, with great thoroughness, so that one enters the communal bathwater spotlessly clean. The local *sento* had recently been modernized and now offered a number of bathing pleasures to help retain its clientele. In the centre was the main bath with very hot water that was just bearable if you slipped in without pause and lay still while your body's temperature adjusted. Along the far wall were smaller, specialized baths: a jacuzzi, a mineral bath, and another which gave the sensation of a mild electric frisson. On the wall near the door was a larger bath that was for me the most memorable. On our first visit, as I was wallowing in the central bath, my sons came over. 'Dad, you must try that bath in the corner. It's sensational!' Unwisely, I took their advice. I plunged in and leapt out with a shriek. It was indeed sensational. It was ice cold.

Back home, we spread out our Japanese bedding, which during the warm season consists of little more than a kind of sheet, called a *towelket*, that absorbs one's sweat. People often say to me that they wish they had a genuine Japanese futon, but little do they realise the complexity of Japanese bedding, and the care with which it must be looked after, not to mention the great space it occupies when folded away during the day. If the day is a sunny one, the futon must not be folded away until it has been aired outside for an hour or two. The weight of one's body compresses the layered cotton of the 'mattress' but the sun and fresh air cause it to expand again. There is, however, a special pleasure in sleeping on a well-aired futon, especially when this is accompanied by the natural scent of the reed-covered *tatami* matting covering the floor.

On that night, as on so many, I enjoyed these Japanese sensations as slowly I eased into sleep, and perhaps into Japanese dreams.

3

Religion

Shinto is the ancient, indigenous religion of Japan. It is thought to have started as a form of nature worship among agricultural communities. Over the centuries it became more and more complex, with various divisions and sects, and theologies that formalized the basic belief in the 'way of the gods'. It was made yet more complex by interaction with Buddhism, Confucianism and Taoism, and lead to the development of architectural styles peculiar to each of the great shrines. Eventually, during the Meiji period, it incorporated emperor worship and Japanese nationalism.

Since the end of the Second World War, the organization of Shinto has been separated from the state, and today it is difficult to tell what Shintoism means to the average Japanese. To most it appears to be more a part of their culture than a matter of faith. Huge crowds flock to the shrines at New Year, and most Japanese babies, swathed in special kimonos, are taken by their parents and paternal grandparents for their 'first shrine visit'. In mid-November the shrines are also full of small children for the Shichi-go-san festival, when children of seven, five and three years old, often clad in traditional Japanese dress, go to give thanks for good health and to receive a bag of special sweets. The festival is particularly colourful at the Heian shrine in Kyoto.

The main shrines themselves are enigmatic, being empty and without a focal point. Around them are other, smaller shrines offering predictions about one's future; a range of amulets offering protection from what may lie in store are also on sale. To the outsider, worship at a shrine appears to be no more than a ritual. But rituals have great significance for the Japanese, at one level meeting a need to 'fulfil the form', and perhaps having a deeper meaning that foreigners cannot understand.

The first time I went to the Grand Shrine at Ise, the most sacred and beautiful of Shinto shrines, I watched the pilgrims with interest. Many had come from afar, and for the many elderly and infirm it involved a strenuous walk from the bus park to the inner shrine. The pilgrims stopped at the outer fence, for only the emperor and the high priest may enter, bowed, gave the ritual handclap, and without pause turned back the way they had come. I shall never know what they were thinking during that brief moment.

The other main religions practised in the country today were brought to Japan at different times. Shamanism came early to Japan, but more importantly, during the Nara period Mahayana Buddhism, Confucianism and Taoism were introduced from China. Under the influence of Prince Shotoku (574–622), Buddhism was promoted as the state religion, while to this day Confucianism has left a deep influence on Japan's social structure.

In the sixteenth century European missionaries and merchants brought Catholicism and Protestantism to Japan. Nobunaga and Hideyoshi, wishing to encourage the trade it brought, protected Christianity. The first Tokugawa shogun, Ieyasu, banned Christianity in 1614 for political reasons and ordered the missionaries to leave the country. Christian missionaries did not return to Japan until after the beginning of the Meiji period, but thereafter both Catholics and Protestants were active, founding churches and universities throughout the country.

A number of what are called 'new religions' developed during the nineteenth and twentieth centuries. Some, like Tenrikyo, were new faiths; others, like Soka Gakkai, were reformed sects of Buddhism, in this case consisting in a revival of the teachings of Nichiren. Several of these 'new religions' were founded by women, some having millions of followers, others only a handful. The followers of the early 'new religions' were persecuted by the government and, during the Meiji period, were forced to become 'sects' of Shinto, though they were able to regain their independence after 1945. It is a complicated story, but without doubt some Japanese have found no spiritual satisfaction in the formalized religions of Shinto and Buddhism and have sought a real faith elsewhere.

This is not, however, the place to attempt a definitive essay on religion in Japan. It may be more illuminating if I describe a few random encounters I have had with some Japanese religions. My observations are largely subjective. I make no apology for that, since religion is the most subjective of human activities.

My first real experience of Buddhism was the most intense. Like many foreigners I became interested in Zen Buddhism, and having read a number of books about it realised that the only way to gain the slightest understanding of Zen was to practise it. Somehow I got myself admitted for one week to Soji-ji, the great training monastery of the Soto sect, just north of Yokohama. It was exactly what I wanted—total immersion. With five hours sleep a night and six forty-five minute sessions of meditation each day, it was hard for a man of forty-three who had never sat in the half-lotus position in his life, but apart from the pain in my legs, it was an exhilarating experience. The atmosphere and life of the monastery were austere but not harsh. More dead than alive, I used to creep to the great communal bath in the evening, where several of the three hundred young monks in training would revive me with massage and good humour. Of course, that week's experience did not bring me within a million miles of enlightenment, but I think it taught me more than reading any number of books would have done, and left a mark on me for the rest of my life.

Later, I spent my first year in Kyoto living in Chotoku-in, a sub-temple of Shokoku-ji, one of the five great Rinzai Zen temples of Kyoto. Here, I was a paying guest, not a Zen postulant. The former priest of Chotoku-in had died some years before and his elder son had succeeded him. But it was his mother, Ogata-san, who really ran the temple, and from the beginning she was running me. She was small and spry, her energy and kindness were equally inexhaustible, and for me it was a wholly enjoyable experience.

At Chotoku-in I was able to observe the daily life of the temple, which in the main is common to all Buddhist sects and to all temples in both large cities and in the country. The role of Buddhism in Japanese life was reduced during the Edo period to looking after the dead, that is, burying them and praying for them. In the Middle Ages Buddhists had cared for the poor and needy, but slowly they were deprived of the performance of such good works and turned into spiritual undertakers.

I have met priests who wished they could make a more vital contribution to their community. I was once spending a night at Temple 2, one of the 88 Temples of the great Shikoku pilgrimage. Just before I was about to go to bed, the priest told me that there would be a short service for the pilgrims at six o'clock the following morning, but it would probably be too early for me. I assured him that I would be present. After the service, and with a smile in my direction, the priest gave a brief address, exhorting the pilgrims to remember other faiths, particularly the spirit of charity in the Christian church which, he said, should be an example to all Buddhist pilgrims.

Chotoku-in had its own burial ground and there were, on average, two memorial services each week while I was living there. The fees the relatives of the deceased paid were the temple's main source of income. The son read the sutras and Ogata-san served tea in a small room to the side of the altar. Memorial services continue to be read for the souls of the departed for fifty years after their death, providing ample work for the priests. Ogata-san would warn me when these services were due and I would turn off my radio and listen to the chanting and the ringing tone of the temple gong.

In addition, I enjoyed Ogata-san's vegetarian cooking and the flower arrangements she put in my room, also the long talks I had with the young priest, and entertaining my students from the nearby campus where I taught. I even learned to tolerate the big spiders I found on my chest when I woke up on hot and sticky summer mornings. Life was both sacred and domestic, but dominated by the sound of the television in the Ogata's quarters.

One day much later, when I was living in a small apartment, the door-bell rang. Two young men stood there, sweating heavily. They asked if they could tell me about the beliefs of Tenrikyo. I said that I should like to hear what they had to say, but I did not want to waste their time. If they were not in a hurry, why didn't they come in and sit down, have a cold drink, and explain Tenrikyo in comfort. The older of the two, Yoshikazu-san, who has since become a close friend, told me later that they had been knocking on doors in Kyoto every day for more than two years and I was the first person who had ever invited them in. Minority religions make the average Japanese person uncomfortable.

Tenrikyo is the largest of the 'new religions'. In 1980 it had 2.5 million followers in Japan, with more overseas, and 16,000 churches around the world. Tenrikyo was founded by a woman, Nakayama Miki (1798–1887), who claimed she had received a revelation from God on 9 December 1838. I have never been able to discover if Miki had read the Bible, but the main elements of her faith partly resemble Christian beliefs. God is the creator of man and, as God the parent, He revealed himself to save men from their selfishness. Miki was born in the village of Shoyashiki, and it is near here that the religion's headquarters, which now occupy much of the town of Tenri, not far from Nara, were later established. There is a vast temple complex built around the *jiba*, the place where it is believed that Miki changed from a human to a spiritual state and where her spirit still resides. I have been to Tenri several times with Yoshikazu-san and have enjoyed eating *mochi* (sticky rice cakes in soup) at the New Year and watching the faithful perform the fascinating and important ritual hand movements of the 'salvation dance service'.

Yoshikazu-san is now the priest of the Tenrikyo church in San Francisco, but by luck we were both in Kyoto in the autumn of 1995, not long after I had broken my leg rather badly. I met him at his Kyoto church and he asked me if I would allow him to perform the healing service for my leg. Later in the day, when we reached Tenri, he asked to perform the service again in front of the *jiba*, so that he might invoke Miki's powers. I cannot gauge the medical value of these acts of faith, but I can say that, as in all my dealings with Tenrikyo, I was deeply touched by his rare kindness and positive religious attitude.

Christianity was first brought to Japan when St Francis Xavier arrived in Kagoshima in August 1549. With the return of Christian missionaries during the Meiji period, every brand of Christianity was brought to Japan. Young Mormons zealously bicycle around every sizeable town offering free English lessons in a form of proselytization. I have known a number of Japanese Christians and have been to a number of Christian services in Japan, and I have always felt that they have reinterpreted the Christian faith to fit their own culture; an opinion borne out by the statements of Japan's famous Catholic novelist, Shusaku Endo. I did, however, find one place in Japan where the spirit of Roman Catholicism was more perfectly observed than in many places in the West.

A few miles from Hakodate, the old southern port of Hokkaido, is Our Lady of the Lighthouse, Japan's famous Trappist monastery, founded by a handful of resolute French monks in the late nineteenth century. The last of the French monks died in the 1950s, by which time there was a well-established Japanese community. The monastery occupies a beautiful position on a plateau of meadowland overlooking the sea, with hills rising behind. The monks lead a simple life, running a large dairy farm producing butter that is sold all over the country. The guest house is shamingly comfortable and the guest master presides over huge and delicious meals. Guests are not required to do anything but would miss much if they did not get up early to hear the monks sing the morning office and the mass, celebrated conjointly by the twelve priests in the community.

In the simple chapel the spirit of La Trappe is perfectly preserved. The services are now sung in Japanese, for which special music was written by a Japanese composer as the Japanese language does not fit traditional Western plainsong. Whatever one's faith, the services are inspiring, but most moving of all is the last moment of the day, after the final office has been sung, when the whole community gathers around the statue of the Virgin and sing in Latin the Salve Regina; an act of faith traditional to Trappist houses around the world. Of all the religious memories I have of Japan, that is the one that remains most vivid in my mind.

4

Tea Drinking

When he classified the plants of the world in the eighteenth century, the Swedish botanist Linnaeus made the mistake of attributing black and green tea to different plants. In fact, all teas commonly called 'China', 'Indian' or 'Japanese' are made from the leaves of the same plant, *Camellia sinensis*. The different colours and flavours are produced by varying the methods of cultivation and processing. The cultivation of tea almost certainly originated in China. Imported Chinese tea had been enjoyed in the great temples of Japan and at the imperial court since the Nara period, but it is probable that the cultivated plant itself was first introduced from China to Japan in 1191 when the Buddhist monk Eisai (1141–1215), founder of the Rinzai sect of Zen, brought back seeds, encouraged its cultivation and extolled its medicinal properties. Eisai's seeds are said to have been planted near Kozan-ji temple, north-west of Kyoto. Wild tea grew in Japan, but it was considered inferior to the tea grown from Eisai's seeds, which was called *honcha*, 'true tea'. Tea was later cultivated in several places. The tea from Uji, south of Kyoto, is considered the finest quality. Today, half of Japan's tea is grown in Shizuoka Prefecture, on the Pacific coast, to the east of Mount Fuji. Everywhere, the leaves on the low, neatly cultivated bushes are picked by women, who fill a small basket they hold in their hand before emptying it into a larger basket tied on the hip.

Japan only produces green tea, which is sold in leaf or powdered form. *Sencha* accounts for 90% of Japanese processed leaf tea. To make it the leaves are steamed to stop fermentation; it is this that keeps them green. Then the leaves are rolled and dried with warm air. *Bancha* is the cheapest green tea, made from older leaves, but processed in the same way. *Gyokuro* is the highest-quality Japanese tea; it is also processed like *sencha*, but made from the finest young leaves. Two other teas, *hojicha* and *kamairicha* are produced by dry-roasting, which makes for a darker and stronger-flavoured tea. *Matcha*, powdered green tea, is used for tea ceremony (as well as sometimes on less formal occasions), and also to flavour such things as ice cream. Like *gyokuro*, it is made from the young leaves, which are steam dried and ground to a fine powder. Hot water is poured on the powder and the mixture is vigorously stirred with a bamboo whisk. *Gyokuro* and *sencha* are brewed with water below boiling temperature, but *bancha* and *hojicha* are made with hotter water. The higher the temperature of the water, the more tannin is infused from the leaf.

For centuries, only powdered green tea was drunk in Japan, and only by the ruling classes. The process for making *sencha* was introduced in the mid-eighteenth century, and *gyokuro* was first produced one hundred years later. It was not until the early twentieth century that mass production of tea made it possible for it to become the national drink of Japan and an integral part of Japanese life. Now every visitor to a home or office is served tea on arrival, and tea is freely available in every restaurant. Office-workers and housewives refresh themselves with tea throughout the day, as do students studying late into the night. Even in the austere world of a Zen monastery, green tea is always available.

The best-quality Japanese teas are sold at Kyoto's famous tea merchants, Ippo-do, founded in 1717. Here one can pay a king's ransom for a large canister of *gyokuro*. As you push your way through the weatherworn, brown canvas *noren*, or half curtains, you enter a shop with long wooden counters, high shelves and a pungent smell—a world of Japanese tea that can have changed little since the Edo period.

The utensils for making, serving and drinking tea, may be seen to reflect Japanese attitudes to their national habit. The large, domestic 'thermos', found in every household, ensures that hot water is always available, and that the small teapot is easily refilled. These 'thermos' have become more and more sophisticated, so that now they have built-in gauges and thermostats and may be plugged into the mains electrical supply. The characteristically delicate floral decoration common on such a functional piece of domestic equipment exemplifies the common desire in Japan to soften the hard edges of reality (see Plate IX).

A tea-set consists of a teapot and five cups, five being the number of every kind of set in Japan. If you want to have more cups, you must buy two sets, but usually the tea-set is only used to serve guests, so five cups are normally sufficient. Saucers are sold separately, and are made of various materials from plain wood to inlaid lacquer. More informally, among the family, tea is drunk from tall 'mugs', often sold in pairs to married couples, one large 'mug' for the man and a smaller one for the woman (see Plate XV). Neither cups nor mugs for Japanese tea have handles, though if you are served Indian or China tea—called *kocha*, 'red tea', and now very popular—or coffee, it will be with a Western-style tea-service with handled cups.

Whatever you are served, your cup will be only two-thirds full, or less. Japanese women in particular drink very slowly and make half a small cup of green tea last a long time. This is considered elegant in a woman. It may be that this way of serving drinks continues a custom developed to help avoid the disaster of spilling liquids on a kimono, or on the *tatami* mats that formerly were used throughout the house. It may also, however, reflect the thriftiness of the Japanese character and a respect for food and drink, which was not always so plentiful as it is today.

Younger women tend to be the pioneers of new tastes in Japan, particularly as they control so many Japanese kitchens and frequent the new Western-style restaurants and coffee shops. Coffee has become enormously popular, among both women and men, and a good Kyoto coffee shop will not only serve delicious coffee but offer a choice of twenty to thirty varieties from around the world. A cup of coffee is expensive, but buying one earns you the right to sit in pleasant surroundings for as long as you wish, as well as an unending supply of glasses of iced water. Japan already produces more tea than it can drink. The time may come when green tea is a minority taste.

5

Tea Ceremony

The origins of the tea ceremony go back to the Zen Buddhist temples of T'ang China (618–907) where a form of tea ritual was performed with special bronze utensils. The monks found that tea helped them stay awake during their long hours of meditation. During the Nara period in Japan, the ceremonial serving of tea was adopted by some of the larger temples. By the Heian period, ritual tea-drinking had become a part of Japanese culture, not only in Buddhist temples, but also among the aristocracy, who collected Chinese utensils and served tea in their pavilions. Despite its Chinese origins, tea ceremony has developed as a uniquely Japanese activity, with spiritual, aesthetic and social elements that make its role in Japanese life difficult to define.

Under the influence of Zen Buddhism, the priestly and aristocratic tea-drinking rituals slowly formalized into what is now called the tea ceremony, known in Japanese as *chanoyu*, meaning 'tea hot-water'. After much of Kyoto had been destroyed during the Onin War in the mid-fifteenth century, the shogun, Ashikaga Yoshimasa, turned his back on this troubled world and retired to his Silver Pavilion, Ginkaku-ji, a complex of fine buildings set around a magnificent garden against the eastern mountains of Kyoto. Here he encouraged the arts and the Noh drama and created what is now called 'Higashiyama Culture'. Under the guidance of a priest named Murata Shuko, a tea ceremony was created that would be recognized as such today.

One of the two original surviving buildings, the Togudo, originally the residence and private chapel of Yoshimasa, has a small, four-and-a-half mat room (about three metres square) where he held tea ceremonies. This is considered the oldest tea-room in Japan, and its dimensions—providing sufficient space for a tea-master and up to five guests—have become the classic model for tea-rooms throughout Japan and wherever else the tea ceremony is performed.

It was, however, Sen no Rikyu (1522–91), who was the founder of the true Japanese ceremony. He formalized the ritual, using a variety of Japanese objects, often of great simplicity. This was inspired by his belief in *wabi*, a refined and elegant aesthetic of simplicity based on a subtle appreciation of nature. Rikyu lived in Kyoto and was tea-master to Oda Nobunaga and Toyotome Hideyoshi, the two military leaders who unified Japan in the second half of the sixteenth century. The tea-master achieved great eminence, but eventually fell into disfavour with Hideyoshi, who ordered him to commit suicide. Rikyu's three great-grandsons each founded a tea-ceremony school: respectively, Ura Senke, Omote Senke and Mushanokoji Senke, the first two of which are today the leading tea-schools in Japan.

There are a great range of tea ceremonies, varying both in the ritual they follow and in their character. There is tea ceremony preceded by a meal, tea ceremony with a charcoal ceremony, tea ceremony with special sweet cakes, with thick tea, with thin tea, and so on. Every movement of the tea-master, including the way he handles the tea utensils (see Plate XXIV), is controlled by an intense discipline of body and mind derived from the spirit of Zen. His movements, however, should not appear controlled but must be fluid and apparently natural. All this takes years of practice. Even the humblest guest must follow an exact ritual that governs when and how to eat the sweet cake, how to receive the tea-bowl from the tea-master, how to drink the tea, how to admire the bowl and, finally, how to return it. And for the foreigner there is a further difficulty. He must be able to sit elegantly on his ankles, Japanese-style, for thirty minutes.

Originally, the tea ceremony was only for men, but during the eighteenth century serving tea became one of the geisha's skills. Today tea ceremony is open to everyone and many good teachers are women. The first tea ceremony I ever attended was in the open air, under an autumn canopy of red, gold and orange maple leaves. Girls in richly decorated autumn kimonos served the thick tea, but the occasion was predominantly a commercial event. A few weeks later in Nagoya the sister of my guide asked us to supper. This was to be my first visit to a private house in Japan. We had an enjoyable family meal, and afterwards Akiko offered to make tea for us. She did it well and, as a good tea-master should, generated a pleasant atmosphere while the family helped me through the ritual performed by each guest. It was an informal ceremony, but there was also a sense of occasion.

Since the Second World War, the leading tea-schools have become very rich, so much so, unfortunately, that money has often seemed to corrupt the true spirit of the 'way of tea'. Teachers pay large sums to be licensed, and students of tea pay large sums for tuition. Encouraged by their parents, who think that possessing the traditional skill will, as the Japanese say, 'gild their daughters for marriage', many girls join their university's tea ceremony club. On occasions, also, great tea-masters perform the tea ceremony—most beautifully no doubt—before large numbers of people who have paid high prices for their tickets. However, I most enjoy simple and private tea ceremonies, which may not be solemn but which are certainly sincere.

My friend Manabu-sensei, a high-school teacher of Japanese and Japanese literature, lives on the island of Shikoku. He is a keen follower of the 'way of tea', and in a corner of his exceptionally large garden he has built a tea-house. In the true spirit of Rikyu, the tea-house contains a four-and-a-half mat room, its design echoes the natural surroundings and everything about it is kept as simple as possible. He likes to use any appropriate utensil, so when he stayed with us in south-west France he bought some simple French pottery bowls to take home to use as tea-bowls. Each time I visit him, he serves tea. I am a clumsy guest, and with most other hosts I feel ill at ease, at Manabu's never. His delightful teacher, a woman, has a gift for putting 'clumsy guests' at their ease. Tea ceremony is always a pleasure there, not solemn, but an activity that, in a quiet and good-humoured way, speaks of the spirit of Zen as, in our various ways, we try to follow 'the way of tea'.

6

Incense

Incense was first brought to Japan from China in the sixth century, with the introduction of Buddhism. It has remained a symbol of purification and, in its commonest form of sticks, it is burnt before the statue of Buddha in temples, and also before the *butsudan*, the domestic Buddhist altar commemorating the ancestors, found in most Japanese homes. In front of some temples there is a large bronze brazier where the faithful stand their smouldering sticks of incense in a bed of ash, drawing the fragrant smoke towards them as a general act of purification or, in some cases, to a particular, afflicted part of the body.

By the eighth century, incense had acquired a secular use, and the rooms and clothes of the nobility were scented by burning incense in the house. For a Heian court lady it became fashionable to have a lingering scent of incense about the person, as described in *The Tale of Genji* and other literature of the Fujikawa period. It was also at this time, a period of extreme refinement at court, that incense competitions became popular. Guests would bring the incense they had made—ground, scented woods and animal scents, mixed with honey—to be judged for the subtlety of their fragrance by the assembled company. Much later, by the late seventeenth century, various forms of 'incense ceremony', complete with strict codes of etiquette and fine utensils, were considered as important as tea ceremony and flower arrangement.

The different ceremonies included such activities as the appreciation of a single scent; trying to identify a particular incense (there are some 2500 kinds); matching one perfume with another; and, most sophisticated of all, combining fragrances to create the atmosphere of a particular passage of literature. There are said to be 700 such blendings, each with its own literary association. Although these incense ceremonies no longer compete with either tea ceremony or flower arrangement, all the equipment, including a small tent supported on a delicate lacquer frame in which the fragrance is isolated, can still be purchased at Kyu-kyodo, Kyoto's famous shop, specializing in calligraphy, paper and incense.

Finally, incense plays a part in that version of the tea ceremony that includes Sumi-demae, the 'Charcoal ceremony', in which fire is prepared for heating the water. During the winter, pottery and porcelain incense boxes, *kogo*, containing small kneaded pellets of incense, are used. In summer, a lacquer box containing three chips of sandalwood incense, *byakudan*, is employed. The principal guest and then the other guests in turn examine the box, after which the tea-master answers questions about the origin of the box and the name of the incense.

There is no better place to study the contemporary manufacture of incense than at Shoeido, a shop in Kyoto founded some 280 years ago by an ancestor of the family who still run it today, eleven generations later. Some chemical ingredients have been added to the process, and modern machinery is now used to make it possible to meet the growing demand. But traditional materials are still essential, ranging from a wide variety of trees and plants, to dried whale meat and the lymph gland of the male Tibetan Jakko deer, the latter now so scarce that a tiny bag of the ingredient may fetch about one million yen (today about £5000).

Incense is made in four forms: sticks, pellets, flakes of scented wood, and a dry powder that may be kept in small brocaded bags tucked into a kimono or in clothes cupboards at home. Incense remains an important part of Japanese secular and religious life. The white-clothed pilgrims making the round of Shikoku's Eighty-Eight Temples—Japan's most important pilgrimage, which symbolizes the life of its most celebrated saint, Kobo Daishi—carry as part of their equipment a special cylindrical tin holding sticks of incense, one of which is burnt at each temple. Incense is one of those elements of Japanese culture that reminds one of the importance of ritual.

The small ceramic incense boxes used at the special tea ceremony may be seen as reflecting several aspects of Japanese life and legend. They are made in every type of ceramic material and in every style (see Plate XVI). Their shape and decoration range from rustic thatched cottages, through animals of the oriental twelve-year cycle—the cock, rabbit, rat, monkey etc., to such everyday objects as cushions and wheels and such seasonal patterns as spring flowers, summer irises and autumn leaves. I was drawn to collect them, as they seemed to me to represent a Japanese world in miniature.

7

Food and Drink

Visitors to Japan often come away with the impression that Japanese food is exceptionally bland and the range of dishes limited. In my opinion, however, Japan's only rival to being able to claim to be the country with the best cuisine in the world, in both quality and variety, is France. Most tourists to Japan get a false impression because they eat mainly in Western-style hotels and restaurants that serve only the sort of Japanese food thought to be suitable for the foreigner's taste; for example, beef dishes like *sukiyaki* or *shabu-shabu*, which were introduced into Japan in modern times and are not part of the authentic tradition of Japanese cooking. Also, few foreigners have the opportunity to eat in Japanese homes, where the style of cooking is quite different from that found in hotels and restaurants. Cost, the language barrier and lack of knowledge prevent the visitor from discovering the marvellous flavours of the full range of Japanese dishes.

Japanese food does tend to be blander than Western food—the Japanese would say more subtle—but there is nothing mild about *natto* (fermented soya beans), *wasabi* (the grated root of horseradish), or a steaming bowl of *ramen* (Chinese noodles), its sauce pungent with garlic. There are dishes for all seasons and all tastes. Traditional Japanese cuisine is based on rice, vegetables and fish, but from early times these have been flavoured with soy sauce, soya bean paste and various herbs. Whatever else, the traditional Japanese diet has given the Japanese people the longest average lifespan in the world; Japanese women can now expect to live to be eighty years old or more.

The variety of Japanese food is reflected in the great number of different tablewares produced, with appropriate dishes for each type of food (see Plates X, XX, XXI and XXVI). It is Japanese practice to serve the whole meal at once; no great effort is made to serve food hot, and hot and cold dishes are served together, though much thought is given to making food look attractive. An everyday meal will consist of rice, today cooked in an electric rice-cooker (Japanese friends are always amazed that I cook my rice in a plain saucepan, a skill they have lost). Rice is served in a small ceramic bowl, soup in a lacquered, or nowadays, plastic bowl with a lid, with some five other side dishes: fish, meat, tofu (bean curd), a variety of vegetables, and Japanese pickles, of which nearly every area in Japan produces its own speciality. My wife's father is especially fond of an aubergine pickle made by a very old pickle shop on the outskirts of Kyoto, and it would be unthinkable for me to visit Kyoto without sending him a packet or two as an *omiagi*, a souvenir from someone travelling.

Traditionally, rice is eaten last, at which point one should stop drinking alcohol; a tradition not always observed nowadays. Each food is served in the appropriate vessel, of suitable shape and relevant decoration. There are dishes for raw fish, *sashimi*, with matching saucers for soy sauce; tall cups with lids for an egg-custard dish, *chawan*; and larger, flat dishes for a whole fish. There are large dishes like the bowl used for a stew, *nabe*, which is ladled into small individual bowls. Japanese kitchens have large cupboards to store all the tableware necessary for the proper serving of a meal.

Since the Second World War, the Japanese culinary tradition has been giving way to convenient and fast Western food so that in Kyoto today there seems to be a hamburger or fried-chicken establishment on nearly every corner. Sadly, this trend seems to be leading to an increase in obesity in the middle-aged and in spotty complexions in the young. One wonders if today's younger generation will live as long as their grandfathers and grandmothers.

Chopsticks have what one might call a culture of their own, though here again the adoption of Western-style cutlery is affecting tradition. Not

Plate XVII. Detail of the lower part of a scroll-painting by Nakajima (nineteenth century) depicting Ushi Matsuri (the Cow Festival) held at Koryu-ji temple every October. This is one of Kyoto's oldest festivals, held at one of Kyoto's oldest temples. (1996.17.190)

Plate XVIII. A scroll-painting by Nikka (died 1845) depicting the Yakasa shrine, popularly known as the Gion shrine. (1996.17.194)

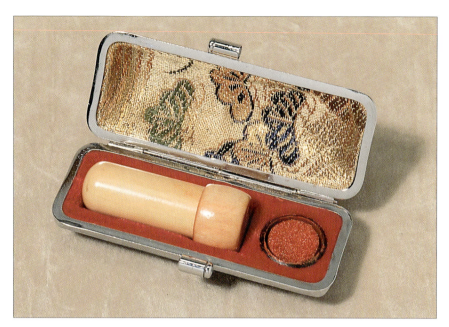

Plate XIX. The author's personal seal, in a case with an ink-pad. (1996.17.131)

Plate XX. Lacquerware and imitation, plastic lacquerware. From front: plastic lidded container, four lacquer coasters for sake bottles, six plastic rice bowls, and six plastic dishes for *o-sushi* or *sashimi*. (1996.17.254, .177, .245 and .242)

Plate XXI. Small porcelain dish, painted with a scene of children playing. (1996.17.227.4)

Plate XXII. Shells with depictions of a mythical emperor and empress; used in a traditional girls' game. (1996.17.140)

Plate XXIII. A set of square porcelain bowls for serving food, with their box. (1996.17.251)

Plate XXIV. Travelling tea ceremony set comprising a tea-whisk, a feather and cloth for cleaning the utensils, a tea-scoop in a brocade case, a porcelain water bottle, a ladle stand, a brocade bag holding the tea container and the tea-bowl, and an incense box. (1996.17.41)

Plate XXV. One of a pair of porcelain sake bottles. (1996.17.175.1)

Plate XXVI. Circular pottery dish from a set for serving *sashimi*, raw fish. (1996.17.250.1)

Plate XXVII. Stoneware bottle from Bizen, one of the oldest kilns in Japan. (1996.17.298)

Plate XXVIII. Square porcelain bottle, painted in underglaze blue. An example of *mingei* work, from the *mingei* shop in Kyoto. (1996.17.265)

Plate XXIX. Envelope for money, given on a celebratory occasion, decorated in the *mizuhiki* style. (1996.17.286)

Plate XXX. Envelope for the 'incense money' given at funerals, decorated in the *mizuhiki* style. (1996.17.287)

Plate XXXI. A new-style of gift envelope designed by Aritaka-san's daughter-in-law to appeal to the younger generation. (1996.17.289)

long ago a Japanese newspaper reported that many recruits to the Japanese police force were so inept with chopsticks that they required special training to master this ancient skill. The chopstick was brought to Japan from China in the eighth century. The Japanese chopstick is shorter and lighter than the Chinese 'ivory' variety. It is normally made of plain pine or cedar wood, or of decorative lacquer over wood.

In the cheapest restaurants you help yourself from a round container full of plain wooden chopsticks, manufactured in one piece and split apart before use. In higher-quality restaurants, the chopsticks come in a paper envelope, often attractively printed with the name and insignia of the establishment. These chopsticks are flat or rounded, and are thrown away after use. Packets of similar chopsticks can also be bought for use at home, but in most families each member has his or her own chopsticks, sometimes kept in a special box. Children use shorter chopsticks, often decorated with images—of the spaceman 'Ultra' for boys, or of the ubiquitous rabbit 'Miffi-chan' for girls—while adults use better-quality plain wooden or lacquered chopsticks.

There are also specialized types of chopstick. There are long chopsticks, some with metal points, for cooking. There are metal chopsticks for arranging charcoal on the fire. There are also the chopsticks used at the crematorium, by the senior male member of the deceased's family, to pick out certain bones from the ashes; notably the thorax, the form of which is thought to resemble that of the seated Buddha.

There is also an etiquette for the use of chopsticks. Even a left-handed person must use his right hand to wield his chopsticks, otherwise the movement of his left elbow will jostle his neighbour. It is rude to point one's chopsticks at anyone. Worse, one must never put them upright in one's food, particularly one's rice bowl, for that is a practice reserved for funerals, at which chopsticks are placed vertically in a bowl of rice before the corpse. Japanese life is full of such traps for the uninitiated. Foreigners can never master every nuance of correct Japanese behaviour, which may explain why so many Japanese are nervous of them.

Kyoto's refined culture has produced several varieties of cooking, though one must go to expensive restaurants, or Buddhist temples, or exclusive tea ceremonies to enjoy them. Kyoto-style cooking, *kyo-ryori*, is generally characterized by subtle rather than strong flavours, and by a fondness for ingredients that give a sense of the seasons. Being situated some way from the sea, Kyoto traditionally depended on vegetables for its cuisine. Even today about thirty special types of vegetable can be bought in the city's famous central market street, Nishiki-koji, which is a living exhibition of Kyoto's characteristic foods.

As Kyoto is the centre of Zen Buddhism, it is not surprising that Zen has exercised a profound influence on many areas of Kyoto life, including cooking. There is thus a style of cooking, *shojin-ryori*, based on the Zen principles of vegetarianism. Even followers of Zen occasionally waive the rules, however, as I found when I was living for a short while in one of the great Zen training monasteries. For example, during the two days before we started an intensive week of meditation some meat was added to our normal vegetable stew so as to strengthen us for the ordeal ahead. The finest Zen-style cooking can be enjoyed without the ordeal at one of the beautiful restaurants around the great Zen temple of Nanzen-ji, the delightful gardens heightening one's enjoyment of the delicate lotus root, tofu, *kudzu* starch and the frothy mountain potato.

Zen has also influenced the light meal sometimes served before tea ceremony. This is known as *kaiseki-ryori, kaiseki* being the stone that a Zen priest puts inside his robe against his stomach to help him bear the pangs of hunger during meditation. *Kaiseki-ryori* is served not for the meal itself, but mainly to prepare the guest for the tea ceremony that follows. Although this meal is extremely light, because of its elegance, the occasion and the general ambience, the Japanese regard it as the height of luxury.

Without doubt, the Japanese enjoy their food. They have their own cooking traditions,

---

Plate XXXII. Ship of Fortune, a masterwork of *mizuhiki* sculpture. Made by Mitsuo Aritaka-san and eight specialist assistants at Iyomishima. Donated by the artist. (1997.18.1)

but ever since the arrival of the Portuguese in the sixteenth century they have borrowed more and more from the Western kitchen, and from other traditions. The most popular cheap dish in Japan today is 'curry rice', though it must be said it is only very distantly related to any Indian original. Many Japanese cooks, however, are master imitators, and Kyoto now boasts French, Italian, Spanish, Mexican, and even an excellent Finnish restaurant. Often the food is adapted to Japanese taste, but I know a tiny French restaurant, run by a Japanese couple, which offers perfect Lyonnaise food, even though, so far as I know, the couple have never been out of Japan.

Finally, I should not like to give the impression that tea-ceremony formality dominates the Japanese table. At home, the wife bustles about, serving more rice with one hand, and picking the children's chopsticks off the floor with the other. Most restaurants are relaxed and welcome children, and the beer flows freely. Wherever you eat, the dominant impression is of a people who appreciate good food. In thirty years of travelling all over Japan, I have had very few poor meals, and many memorable ones. When I return to Kyoto, it takes me more than a week to visit all my favourite restaurants, most of which are very cheap and all of which are good by any standard.

In Japan, food is inseparable from drink. The national drink, sake, has in recent years retreated before the growing popularity of Japan's excellent light beers. A cheaper spirit, *shochu*, sometimes flavoured with fruit juice, is popular among young people, while both imported and Japanese wines have grown in popularity, particularly among women. Among men Scotch whisky and brandy remain prestigious drinks, particularly in the small bars found in their hundreds in such entertainment districts as Gion in Kyoto. Drunkenness is not common but is no disgrace, providing that you are back at your desk in the office the following morning. It says much for Japan's high standard of public behaviour that even though every kind of alcohol, including bottles of wine and whisky, may be purchased from dispensing machines twenty-four hours a day, this does not result in the sort of drunkenness and vandalism that one might expect in almost any other country in the world.

In the southern part of Kyoto is a district called Fushimi that has excellent water and, as a result, is one of the two most famous sake-brewing areas in Japan. Sake is brewed by large and small companies all over Japan, and every keen sake-drinker has his favourite kind. After the Second World War, the general standard of sake brewing sank to a low level, with many brewers being out to make a quick profit by using only second-rate ingredients. As happened in Britain with the 'real ale' movement, there was a consumer reaction and a new demand for good sake, which encouraged many small breweries to open. Today, the choice of kinds of sake is much wider and the quality higher.

The essential ingredients for sake are pure water and a special kind of good-quality rice. In the brewing of sake, temperature control is critical. In the old breweries there were long rows of windows past which an experienced brewer raced, opening and closing them as his judgement dictated. Once, the chief scientist at the Gekkeikan brewery showed me the modern computer-controlled methods of manufacture. He then opened a bottle of a wonderful premium-quality sake; it tasted like a fine German wine and cost more than one hundred dollars a bottle. He also told me that the practice of warming sake was usually disastrous and that every day a huge proportion of the sake drunk in Japan is spoilt by overheating.

This is borne out by the practice of my only Japanese friend who is knowledgeable about sake. He always serves it cold and in a glass tumbler. Not for him the charming but minuscule cups and their accompanying sake bottles (see Plate XXV). The majority, however, like the social ritual of small cups and the necessity of refilling your neighbour's cup over and over again. There is a nice old Edo saying about sake drinking: 'The sake should be warm, the cuisine *sashimi*, and the pourer a beautiful woman.' However, 'warm' does not mean hot.

8

Paper

There are two shops in Kyoto that stock the full range of the modern art of *washi*, Japanese handmade paper. Their walls are lined with deep shelves stocked with dozens of different sorts and colours of handmade paper in dozens of different colours. These papers are now expensive, for the process of making them is long, laborious and slow. Despite the high prices, there still seems to be considerable demand for *washi* in all its forms.

It is known that papermaking was introduced to Japan from China. Exactly when is uncertain, though it was certainly well-established by the Nara period. Since then, and in a variety of ways, *washi*, as distinct from *yoshi*, Western paper, has become an important part of Japanese culture. Handmade paper is still made in many places in Japan, and there are also a number of paper museums. Since the Nara period, paper-makers have produced a great variety of papers—of different textures, colours and with various decorations—for different purposes.

Japanese paper-makers use the natural fibres from three plants: *mitsumata* and *gampi*, which are indigenous, and the inner bark of the paper mulberry tree. By a laborious process of steaming, soaking in water and beating, the pulp is produced. In a process unique to Japan, the pulp is then suspended in a solution of taro-like starch, *tororo aoi*. The fibrous liquid is picked up in a meshed rectangular mould, which is gently shaken from side to side to entangle the floating fibres. When the paper-maker judges that the sheet will hold together, he lifts it off the mould and puts it on top of the pile of drying sheets. Later, the moisture is pressed out of the pile, and the sheets of paper are peeled off and dried separately on pine planks or metal sheets. The paper may be coloured during this process by the addition of dyes or other plant material. Every time I stand by the maker and watch the liquid turn into a solid piece of paper it seems to me that I am witnessing a small miracle.

Because of its fibrous structure, Japanese paper is extremely strong. It is used for a great variety of products, even for garments, and it plays a vital part in traditional architecture. For example, the two types of sliding partitions that divide up the space in Japanese homes—the sliding screens, *fusuma*, and the translucent windows, *shoji*—are made of paper. There are also a variety of papers for calligraphy and painting, as well as modern-style stationery made from attractively decorated papers. Wallets and purses are made of particularly strong paper, while paper is also used for traditional lanterns, for bamboo-and-paper light fittings in traditional designs, and for a variety of boxes, oiled-paper umbrellas, and both folding, *sensu*, and rigid, *uchiwa*, fans.

The Japanese fascination with paper is demonstrated by the art of origami, which of course is now known and practised around the world. Origami can be used for making delicate toys and dolls and is related to the Japanese gift for both practical and attractive wrapping. When purchasing anything traditional, and certainly when purchasing anything suitable for a gift—from incense to boxes of cakes—one may find elements of origami folding in the wrapping. Indeed, all shop assistants used to be skilled in wrapping even the most ordinary of parcels. I remember making purchases at department stores in Tokyo during my first years in Japan and watching the assistants make beautiful parcels. I would return to my hotel eager to examine my purchases more closely, but would be unable to bring myself to destroy the beautiful wrapping. In the end, I usually took the parcels back to England unopened. Sadly, this once universal skill is disappearing and department-store packaging is not the art it used to be.

9

Calligraphy and Seals

I must begin this chapter with a cautionary tale, which is also a story against myself. Many years ago I was leading a party of English and American visitors on a cultural tour of Japan. Among the many special attractions was a visit to the beautiful Yamato Bunkakan Museum, near Nara, which has a superb collection of Far Eastern art, including a number of Japanese masterpieces. I failed to do my homework properly, so that we arrived expecting a feast of painting and sculpture but found instead an exhibition devoted solely to examples of Japanese calligraphy. The centrepiece of this high-quality exhibition, presented in a reverential setting, was a document written by an early Japanese emperor. I struggled to enthuse about this masterpiece, but in all honesty it meant no more to me than a hastily written imperial laundry list. The true appreciation of calligraphy is not easy for the ignorant Westerner, any more than mastering the art itself is.

The Japanese have long had the highest regard for calligraphy, which for them is not just the writing of characters but a disciplined art, closely related to poetry and painting. Even today, all schoolchildren learn basic calligraphy and a good calligraphic style is a sign of a cultivated man, though the skill is growing rarer. This interest in writing 'their own language' spills over into analysis of how foreigners pen their own languages, and I have often heard Japanese appreciate attractive Western handwriting.

Calligraphy is certainly an art. I used to enjoy going to the Kitano shrine in northern Kyoto at New Year, where small children sat solemnly struggling to produce 'the first writing'. I found their sprawling, spidery characters very sympathetic. They were just like mine; but I am left-handed and I shall never master Japanese calligraphy. A friend spent a morning trying to teach me, but in the end he said, 'If you really want to learn calligraphy, first you must learn to do it with your right hand. Otherwise, your brush strokes will always be going in the wrong direction.' And when I come to think about it, I have never met a left-handed Japanese person, nor anyone who complained about having to make the change from left-hand to right.

To practice *shodo*, 'the Way of writing', one needs a brush, *fude*, and Chinese ink, *sumi*. Normally, one also buys a writing box and equips it with an inkstone on which to mix the ink, two thick brushes and two slender brushes, a ceramic water-dropper, and a small weight to hold down the top of the paper, the bottom being secured by the left hand. One also needs a large quantity of thin and slightly absorbent paper on which to practise. The beginner finds it difficult to control the size and proportions of each character (some characters are composed of over forty strokes, each of which must be executed in the correct order), and he is helped by a felt pad placed under the sheet of paper. On one side of the pad are large squares to contain the beginner's efforts. After gaining some control, the calligrapher turns the felt pad over to the side covered with smaller squares within which he must now contain the characters. After considerable practice, the pad is put away. The control of the brush, which is held almost upright, largely depends on the strength of the wrist. I have to say that it is one of those activities that is far harder than it looks.

Japan had no written language until it adopted Chinese writing in about the fifth century AD. Soon the Japanese began to adapt the Chinese characters, *kanji*, to the structure of their own language, inventing an additional phonetic 'alphabet', *hiragana*, to deal with the intricacies of Japanese grammar. There is a second syllabic writing form, *katakana*, which is also old but nowadays used mainly for writing foreign names. It is possible to write Japanese entirely in *kana*, without using Chinese characters, and this was how the great women writers of the Heian period, including Lady Murasaki, wrote their masterpieces, because at that time women were not allowed to study Chinese. Today, children start by learning to read and write *hiragana*, and go on to master some 2500 Chinese characters by the time they leave school at the age of eighteen. An extremely literate Japanese professor might know about 6000 characters.

Over the centuries, various styles of calligraphy have been developed and admired, and it is quite common, particularly for tea ceremony, to hang a scroll of fine Zen calligraphy instead of a scroll painting as an object of aesthetic contemplation. A work of fine calligraphy by a famous master can fetch a great deal of money. I was once in Kyoto with the great American collector, Philip Hofer, on his last buying excursion at the age of eighty. He wanted to make one final spectacular purchase and we went to see Kyoto's leading art dealer, Takashi Yanagi. After the necessary interval for tea and politenesses, Yanagi-san produced a small scroll and unrolled it with care. It was the work of another emperor, but this time even I could see that it was a thing of great distinction. I knew Philip very well and I knew that he was going to buy it, whatever the price. The dealer quoted a price of sixteen million yen. I knew that Philip was not going to pay that, and I suspected that Yanagi-san also knew it. When it came to bargaining, Philip was the wiliest of foxes. He went into one of his routines: devious, emotional and outrageous. How could Yanagi ask him such a price; an old customer, indeed, an old friend? And didn't Yanagi-san know he was an old man? And worse, he had recently lost his wife in the most tragic circumstances (this was true). Crocodile tears began to pour down Philip's cheeks. The two men settled on fifteen million yen.

There have been, and still are, movements in Japan that favour getting rid of the Chinese characters and using the Western alphabet instead. This has not received general support, although since the Second World War the government has simplified *kanji* to some extent. Most Japanese are convinced that giving up *kanji* would undermine Japanese culture. That is possibly true, though equally it might help Japan to join the community of nations. There are, however, many who positively enjoy the protection of the language barrier, and perhaps some who want the next generation to suffer, as they did, having to master *kanji*. Learning *kanji* takes up a considerable proportion of the school curriculum. While it does tend to give Japanese schoolchildren good visual memories, the time it takes to learn it deprives them of the opportunity to study other subjects.

Modern technology has made life easier. When I first went to work for Seibu, a large Japanese company, in 1967, everything had to be written by hand since there was in those days no practical typewriter for writing *kanji*. There was one clumsy machine with a moveable arm and a huge bed of moveable typeface, each piece producing a single *kanji* character. The operator moved the arm to pick up the required character, which was then swung over the paper and printed. It was a laborious business. Computerized typewriters and word-processors have speeded up the process, but it is still more complicated than working with the Roman alphabet. While several thousand characters can be stored in the 'memory', they cannot all be assigned keys. So one must search through the phonetic *hiragana* for the character one needs, probably finding that the sound you type in *hiragana* produces several *kanji* characters on the screen, from which you must then choose the one you require.

There is also the world of seals, *hanko*. Every adult needs two seals: an informal one for signing receipts for deliveries and similar simple transactions (see Plate XIX); and an official seal, which must be registered, for more formal transactions. Written signatures are acceptable from foreigners, who may not have a registered seal, but they are not legal for Japanese. If a foreigner has an informal seal, it should be written in *katakana*, the phonetic alphabet for all foreign names. Beyond the strictly personal seals, there are also official seals and some specially cut for particular purposes. It was in this area that I once made a complete fool of myself.

I had started collecting Japanese books and

maps, in particular old guide books to Kyoto. Though I did not know if Japanese book collectors had seals equivalent to Western bookplates, I thought I should like to mark each book I bought with an appropriate Japanese seal. One day I was having lunch in Kyoto with an old friend who knew a great deal about Japanese crafts. I asked her about having a seal cut for my books. She said that it was possible, and that she knew of a well-known seal-cutter in Kyoto who specialized in that kind of seal. I suggested that we should visit him after lunch. She look horrified. It was out of the question. It would take months to establish the right rapport. I must start visiting him once a week, watching him work, admiring his seals, seeking his favour, but never actually mentioning that I wanted him to cut a seal. After months of this, when I sensed the moment had come, I might suggest that I was interested in a seal, though I had no idea if he would have the time to undertake such trifling work.

I gave up at that point, partly because I sensed that such a rigmarole would certainly result in a bill I could not afford, and secretly because, as far as I was concerned, I thought that my friend was talking rubbish. I am sure that this is how she would have gone about it, but I was equally certain that if I had gone to see him the next day and asked him to cut the seal, he would have agreed immediately. That is the privilege of being a foreigner in Japan. One can make the direct approach, or the direct statement, and get away with it. Japanese friends often say to me, 'I don't know how you can be so daring,' when I am completely unaware that I have done anything at all unusual.

10

Mingei

The *mingei* movement, to protect and promote Japanese folk crafts, was founded by Munoyoshi Yanagi (1896–1961). Working at the time in Korea, then a colony of Japan, he began by studying and collecting the folk crafts, particularly the ceramics, of the Yi dynasty (1393–1910), and later founded a museum in Seoul based on his own collection. At the same time he developed a personal aesthetic philosophy focused on folk crafts or *mingei*, the concept of which he first developed in 1926. Yanagi had studied European art but reacted against the Western emphasis on the creativity of the individual artist, believing that the beauty of craft objects came from the anonymity of the tradition and the special relationship between the craftsman and the user. His views were influenced by his Buddhist belief that a reliance on the mercy of the Buddha was more important in gaining salvation than personal effort. Yanagi was a philosopher and an idealist and saw machines as damaging, particularly to rural communities.

Yanagi attracted various followers, best-known among whom was the potter Shoji Hamada. Together they founded in 1936 the Japan Folk Craft Museum at Komaba, near Tokyo. Research was carried out into Japanese folk crafts, resulting in the publication of Yanagi's *Handicrafts in Japan* in 1972. In 1927, Yanagi had attempted to establish a craft commune in Kyoto, but it soon failed. In 1934 the Japan Folk Craft Society was founded as the central organization of the *mingei* movement and shops were established in the main cities throughout Japan to support *mingei* artists by selling their work. There are two of these shops in the centre of Kyoto, one specializing in ceramics, basketwork and glass, the other specializing in furniture and furnishings. My friend Tsune Sesoko, who worked as Yanagi's assistant during the Second World War, has pointed out that by their nature and their extremely high prices the objects now sold in the *mingei* shops have little to do with Yanagi's own ideas.

I had one experience with the *mingei* shop in Kyoto that certainly ran counter to the importance Yanagi placed on the relationship between the craftsman and the user. When visiting the shop one day I found four handsome square plates. Four was not a practical number for me, but as the shop had no more of them the assistant telephoned the potter who had made them. Unfortunately, he had none in stock either, but he promised he would be making some more of that particular type of plate within a few months. I bought the four plates and left an order for four more. (I should add that they were very expensive, which also runs contrary to Yanagi's view that *mingei* consists in humble objects for ordinary people.) I let the matter rest for several months, then returned to collect the other four plates. They had not arrived, and when the assistant again telephoned the potter, he said he had decided not to make any more. When I told Tsune Sesoko, who is rather cynical about modern *mingei*, all she said was, 'How typical!'

At the heart of Yanagi's teaching was the belief that work should not be signed and that the craftsman should remain anonymous and be content to live within the reputation of his craft's tradition. This has led to considerable hypocrisy. I remember visiting Hamada, who never signed his pots, at Mashiko, sitting on the ground by his side, talking all day while he decorated large plates. At the end of the day, he took me to a small building where there were shelves full of his work and invited me to choose for myself any piece I liked. I chose a vase with much the same flower pattern as the one he had been putting on the plates. I thanked him, then teasingly held out a pencil and the vase and asked him to sign it. He smiled. 'You know I never sign my work,' he said. I would have liked to reply, 'Quite true, but you frequently sign the boxes you sell your pieces in, which adds enormously to their value.'

Yanagi failed to realise that genuine craft traditions will only survive, rather than turn into production for collectors and souvenir hunters, if there is an indigenous market for their products. The pottery Yanagi admired in Korea, and later in Japan, was made by local potters for local people, and there was indeed genuine inspiration to be found both in the tradition itself and in the discipline of practicality. A traditional craft cannot flourish, however, unless its products are still used for their original purposes. There are some traditional Japanese crafts, particularly in Kyoto, which have retained their identity because they are still genuinely in use. *Mingei* lost its way. Unfortunately, however, the craftwork that Yanagi admired so deeply and wanted so passionately to preserve through his *mingei* movement became separated from the main traditions of Japanese craftsmanship.

11

Mizuhiki

When one begins to travel about Japan, many traditional objects, still in everyday use, catch the eye and make one wonder what they are for. In every stationery shop, for example, one sees a large rack of brightly coloured envelopes, wrapped around with what appears to be coloured string, tied in a flat, ornamental knot (see Plates XXIX–XXXI). Some of these envelopes are sombre, tied with black-and-white strings, but most are red-and-white, with origami folding, and bear a profusion of gold and silver decoration. These all seem to be in a traditional style, but alongside them are a range of prettier envelopes, in pastel pinks and blues, their strings tied to form delicate bouquets. These, it turns out, are designed to please the shopper with less traditional tastes; in Japan it is the young girls who have money to spare.

All such envelopes are bought to contain gifts of money, which is given on a variety of occasions in Japan and must always be wrapped. The sombre, black-and-white envelopes are to hold the 'incense money' given to the widow at a funeral to help defray the cost. The colourful envelopes, often with knots in the form of a turtle or a crane, are for birthdays, weddings and other occasions at which money is the appropriate gift. I had been familiar with these matters for a long time and had occasionally bought an envelope for a friend's birthday gift, or for one of my students' weddings, but it was a long time before I realised that they formed an important part of the traditional craft of *mizuhiki*. The word itself means 'water drawn', referring to the way in which the 'strings' are made

When I was staying on Shikoku Island with some friends who lived just outside the famous paper-making town, Iyomishima, they told me that amidst the great factories mass-producing household papers, there was the workshop of a well-known *mizuhiki*-maker, Aritaka-san. It was often in just this sort of way that I stumbled on a Japanese craft new to me and had the unexpected opportunity to visit a workshop previously unknown to me. As elsewhere in the world, some of Japan's most distinguished craftsmen work in small suburban houses or obscure back streets. As we arrived at Aritaka-san's workshop, I expected to find him making gift envelopes, so the more spectacular aspects of the craft of *mizuhiki* I witnessed there took me completely by surprise.

First, however, Aritaka-san took us to another building where the 'strings' essential to all *mizuhiki* are made. Here, long, narrow bands of a strong white paper were tightly twisted to form a 'string', which was then impregnated with a fine white clay mixed with glue. When dry this paper string is as strong and pliable as a thin cord and can be dyed, silvered, gilt or, in a recent development, coated in fluorescent rainbow colours created in high-tech laboratories in Kyoto. These coloured 'strings'—usually associated with the gift envelopes, but in fact only introduced to that craft at the end of the Second World War—were first used for the older craft of *mizuhiki* sculpture.

The paper strings were first developed by a papermaker called Bunhichi in a papermaking town called Iida, in Nagano Prefecture, around the mid-eighteenth century. At first the 'strings' were popular for tying hair, being a cheap substitute for *himo* or braided cords. During the Meiji period, however, Western hairstyles became popular. As a consequence only two *mizuhiki*-makers survived in business, at Iida and Iyomishima, while *mizuhiki*-work took an entirely new form.

Especially in rural communities, it had long been the practice at engagement celebrations for the *tokonoma*, or alcove in the main room, to be decorated with various objects symbolizing good luck, wealth and long life. Originally, these objects had been made of rice-straw but the *mizuhiki* craftsmen developed an elaborate and charming form of sculpture, braiding, weaving and binding the 'strings' into various auspicious objects: sprays of plum, bamboo and pine; large prawns, cranes and turtles; figures representing a long-married couple; and in a crescendo of colour and skill, the Ship of Fortune, bales of rice piled high behind the dragon prow.

Aritaka-san has generously given a large version of the Ship of Fortune, his masterwork, to the Pitt Rivers Museum (see Plate XXXII). It was made with the help of eight assistants and he tells me he may never make such a large ship again. Indeed, the ship now in the Pitt Rivers Museum is one of only two such large versions ever created. The other one was given to the French government and was exhibited at Charles de Gaulle airport. Although it may be hard to believe, this elaborate boat, like all the other engagement sculpture, is made entirely from *mizuhiki* strings. Engagement sets come in a variety of forms and at a range of prices, and it is also possible to rent a set for the ceremony. In towns all over Japan there are small shops selling and renting them, but only the very grandest set would include a Ship of Fortune.

When the engagement is finalized, the man's family brings the set to the girl's home and pays the bridal gift. This is the money—equivalent to about a quarter of the groom's annual salary—given to the bride-to-be so that she may buy in advance the furniture for the new home, though part of the cost will be met by her own family. Both sides are anxious that the payment shall in no way appear to represent the bride's price so the *mizuhiki* set is used to dress up the gift and to emphasize its true purpose. At the centre of the display is a wooden tray holding a gorgeously decorated envelope containing the money. This is accompanied on a second tray by a notional inventory, in another elaborate envelope, of the furniture to be bought. These may be accompanied by a third envelope with a gift of money for the *nakodo*, the formal sponsor of the engagement and marriage. It should be stressed that what I have given here is only a basic account of what can be a far more complicated procedure, varying from region to region.

The objects for the engagement ceremony represent about 30% of the total business and the decorated envelopes the other 70%. The envelopes also vary from region to region. For example, the envelopes from Kanto and Kansai are folded differently, a difference that may derive from the styles of Iida and Ishinomiya respectively. In Tokyo taste is restrained; 'even thrifty', said Aritaka-san's son with a smile. Kansai people like more elaborate decoration, this taste reaching a crescendo of opulence in Hiroshima, whose inhabitants demand a gorgeous display of gold and silver knots with sprays of trembling filigree flowers.

To stay in business, the *mizuhiki*-maker must sustain and expand his market with innovations. Aritaka-san's daughter-in-law, a creative and energetic person, has designed a range of prettier cards, in which the traditional knots are replaced by delicate flower sprays, to capture the market of the fashion-conscious young (see Plate XXXI). Only the other day I saw an article about her in a Japanese magazine showing how she is now developing the art of *mizuhiki* strings into a form of flower arrangement. In the world of contemporary Japanese crafts such innovations help to sustain traditional work.

12

A Last Glimpse

Most of the recollections that make up the text of this book relate to the years I lived in Kyoto between 1978 and 1991. I first visited the city in 1967, and I have been back in the last few years, but those thirteen years make up the heart of my experience. Often when I look back now, I try to judge how much Kyoto has changed during the past thirty years; in its general appearance and its daily life, and in the expressions of its traditional culture. Perhaps because absence had given me a more objective eye, during my most recent stay in the autumn of 1995 I thought I detected a considerable change.

Somehow Kyoto has become a harder city. This is reflected in its new architecture. Nobody can miss the new Kyoto Hotel, exactly in the centre of the city, and the first building in the city to be allowed to rise seven further storeys above the long-established limit of seven storeys. Now, inevitably, more and more new buildings will rise to such a height, destroying the quality that contributed so much to the character of Kyoto when I first went there: a clear view of the eastern hills from almost anywhere in the centre of the city. I can forgive the new Kyoto Hotel its soulless architecture. I cannot forgive the fact that it has blocked out another large segment of the view of those green hills that brought such refreshment to those walking the streets of the city.

There are other public buildings, some put up to celebrate Kyoto's twelve-hundredth anniversary in 1994, which are not so much works of architecture as municipal statements; though of what I am not certain. I can only describe the Kyoto International Community House and the Museum of Kyoto, undistinguished as they are both outside and inside, as two monumental white elephants. And on the street there is appalling traffic, serious pollution, and the daily warfare waged on the pavements between aggressive cyclists and intransigent pedestrians.

Change is difficult to measure, particularly in Japan where it is often so imperceptible, but I do not think that I would want to live in Kyoto now. That must, however, reflect a change in me as well as in Kyoto. Special places have their own time in one's life.

Yet when I think again, and think of other aspects of Japanese life, I wonder if anything has changed at all. Every day last autumn I went to shop at my favourite covered market, Demachi, where I have shopped since 1978. The same shops were still there and I recognized a few of the shopkeepers, including the energetic man who runs the cheap fruit stall around the corner. The whole place was as vital, cheerful and cheap as it ever had been. The stationery shop still stocked a great variety of *mizuhiki* envelopes, and the clothes shop still displayed a stock of that intriguing old-fashioned underwear by which Japanese men and women attempt to keep themselves cool in summer and warm in winter.

I went to Kyoto in 1978 to teach, and to write a book about fourteen crafts, twelve of them traditional to Kyoto. In selecting the crafts for the book, one of my criteria was that the objects themselves must still be in daily use and be found in any Japanese house. Even by that date, some crafts were beginning to look to be in danger of becoming extinct. I thought that the special Kyoto broom was most at risk, and indeed there were only two craftsmen left who could make this elaborate type of broom. But the real danger for the craft, as the broommaker Ishikawa-san explained, was that there was only one shop left in Kyoto, at the west end of Sanjo bridge, which specialized in traditional brushes and brooms. Ishikawa-san said that the shop now sold only a tenth of what it had sold twenty-five years earlier, and that it would close when the old woman who ran it died. It was a fascinating shop, over two hundred years old, and during my autumn visit, I went to see it if was still open. It was, though there was no sign of the old woman, and a younger women seemed to be in charge (see Plate III). That is Japan. I doubt if it will ever be allowed to close. From huge companies to dusty corner shops, once an institution becomes part of Japanese history and tradition, some unseen force ensures that it continues.

But what of the younger generation? When I read the stories of Banana Yoshimoto, I catch a glimpse of an entirely new Japanese world. Last week, a Japanese friend was telling me that far fewer girls than in the past now join their university tea ceremony club. And when I observe the young children of my Japanese friends, I do not quite see how they are going to make the cultural leap from soccer and computer games back into traditional Japanese life. But if I have learned anything about Japan during my life in Kyoto, it is not to make predictions about the future direction of Japanese life.

Suggested Further Reading

Some of the works in this list have been published in various editions. Only details of the most recent or the most accessible editions are given here.

By the author

Japanese Crafts (photographs by Mark Lowe), London: John Murray, 1983.

Into Japan, London: John Murray, 1985.

A Short Guide to the Kyoto Museum of Archaeology, Kyoto: Kyoto Museum of Archaeology, 1991.

'Letter from Kyoto', in *The American Scholar*, Vol. LXII, no. 4, Autumn 1993, pp. 571–9.

History

Charles James Dunn, *Everyday Life in Traditional Japan*, Tokyo: Charles E. Tuttle, 1981.

Seiichi Iwao (ed.), *Biographical Dictionary of Japanese History* (translated by Burton Watson), Tokyo: International Society for Educational Information.

Ivan Morris, *The World of the Shining Prince: Court Life in Ancient Japan*, Tokyo: Charles E. Tuttle, 1978.

Herbert E. Plutschow, *Historical Kyoto*, Tokyo: Japan Times, 1983.

Richard Ponsonby-Fane, *Kyoto: The Old Capital of Japan*, Kyoto: The Ponsonby Memorial Society, 1956.

Guide books

Japan: The New Official Guide, Tokyo: Japan Travel Bureau, 1991.

John H. Martin and Phyllis G. Martin, *Kyoto: A Cultural Guide to Japan's Ancient Imperial City*, Rutland, Vermont: Tuttle, 1994.

Must-See in Kyoto, Tokyo: Japan Travel Bureau, 1985.

Gouverneur Mosher, *Kyoto: A Contemplative Guide*, Rutland, Vermont: Tuttle, 1978.

Martin Roth and John Stevens, *Zen Guide: Where to Meditate in Japan*, New York: Weatherhill, 1985.

Shiro Usui, *A Pilgrim's Guide to Forty-Six Temples* (translated by Stephen D. Miller), New York: Weatherhill, 1990.

Novels

Yasunari Kawabata, *Beauty and Sadness* (translated by Howard Hibbett), Rutland, Vermont: Tuttle, 1991.

Yasunari Kawabata, *The Old Capital* (translated by J. Martin Holmes), Rutland, Vermont: Tuttle, 1991.

Yukio Mishima, *The Temple of the Golden Pavilion* (translated by Ivan Morris), Harmondsworth: Penguin, 1987.

Junichiro Tanizaki, *The Makioka Sisters* (translated by Edward G. Seidensticker), Rutland, Vermont: Tuttle, 1984.

Eiji Yoshikawa, *The Heike Story* (translated by Fuki Wooyenaka Uramatsu), Rutland, VT: Tuttle, 1988.

Reference Works

Kodansha Encyclopaedia of Japan (9 volumes), Tokyo: Kodansha, 1983.

Kyoto–Osaka: A Bilingual Atlas, Tokyo: Kodansha, 1992.

About the Author

After reading English at New College, Oxford, John Lowe worked in the departments of woodwork and ceramics, and later as assistant to the Director, at the Victoria & Albert Museum. He was Director of Birmingham Museum and Art Gallery, founding director of the Weald & Downland Open Air Museum, and founding principal of West Dean College. Later he was Visiting Professor in British Cultural Studies at Doshisha University, Kyoto. Since 1982 he has been a professional writer. Among his books are *Thomas Chippendale, Cream Coloured Earthenware, Japanese Crafts, Into Japan, Into China, Corsica, Edward James: A Surrealist Life,* and *The Warden: A Portrait of John Sparrow* (forthcoming). He was a major contributor to the *Encyclopaedia Britannica* and the *Oxford Junior Encyclopaedia*, and is the author of some 200 articles about furniture, ceramics, stained glass, foreign travel, English, American and Japanese literature, and many aspects of Japanese culture. He is a Fellow of the Society of Antiquaries.